21st
Century
Skills Library

COOL CAREERS

ORGANIC FARMER

TAMRA B. ORR

Published in the United States of America by
Cherry Lake Publishing, Ann Arbor, Michigan
www.cherrylakepublishing.com

Content Adviser
Darrell Frey, Three Sisters Farm

Credits
Photos: Cover and page 1, ©Wildscape/Alamy; page 4, ©Gvictoria/Dreamstime.com;
page 7, ©Darkop/Dreamstime.com; page 8, ©Pakhnyushcha, used under license from
Shutterstock, Inc.; page 11, ©Palto, used under license from Shutterstock, Inc.; page 12,
©Orientaly/Dreamstime.com; page 14, ©Daniel Dempster Photography/Alamy;
page 17, ©Moth/Dreamstime.com; page 18, ©Nataliua/Dreamstime.com; page 20,
©Anthony Harris, used under license from Shutterstock, Inc.; page 23, ©Jim
West/Alamy; page 24, ©Mazor/Dreamstime.com; page 26, ©Benjamin Volant/
Alamy; page 27, ©Wayne HUTCHINSON/Alamy

Library of Congress Cataloging-in-Publication Data
Orr, Tamra.
  Organic farmer / by Tamra B. Orr.
    p. cm.—(Cool careers)
  Includes index.
  ISBN-13: 978-1-60279-500-6
  ISBN-10: 1-60279-500-2
  1. Organic farming—Vocational guidance—Juvenile literature.
  2. Organic farmers—Juvenile literature. I. Title. II. Series.
  S605.5.O77 2010
  631.5'84023—dc22   2008047264

Cherry Lake Publishing would like to acknowledge
the work of The Partnership for 21st Century Skills.
Please visit *www.21stcenturyskills.org* for more information.

ORGANIC FARMER

TABLE OF CONTENTS

CHAPTER ONE
AN APPLE A DAY—OR NOT

Emily Hall yawned as she packed her son's lunch box for school. She filled it with a peanut butter and jelly sandwich and a small bag of potato chips. Then she added a

Many people were surprised that an apple could be a threat to their health.

red apple and a small box of apple juice. It was Justin's favorite lunch.

As she put his lunch together, Emily flipped on the television. A news reporter was talking. Behind him was a picture of an apple orchard. Puzzled, Emily turned up the sound.

"Alar is a chemical sprayed on much of the world's apple supplies to make sure they ripen at the same time. But Alar has been shown to cause lung and kidney cancer in mice," the reporter stated. "According to experts, it is being pulled off the shelves. The company that makes it has halted production until further studies have been made. In the meantime," he continued, "doctors are reminding everyone that a person would have to eat huge quantities of apples to be at risk. In fact, you would have to drink thousands of quarts of apple juice every day!"

Frowning, Emily looked inside her son's lunch box. She reached in and pulled out the apple and the juice box. She replaced them with a banana and a bottle of water. Until she knew more about Alar, Justin's favorite lunch would have to change.

This apple scare happened in 1989. A news report about the possible dangers was shown on television's *60 Minutes*. The reaction was immediate. Parents threw away bags of apples and jugs of juice. Apples were taken off grocery store shelves. The public began demanding to know more about what was happening. Was their food safe? Because of the evidence about its dangers, the Uniroyal Chemical Company had to halt the production of Alar.

It was not the first time that a dangerous chemical had been used on America's food supplies. It was not the last time either. But it did point out the need to change how food was grown and produced. It also helped advance the idea of organic farming. Organic farmers grow food without hurting the environment. They don't use dangerous chemicals.

Sir Albert Howard was the pioneer of organic farming. He was raised on a farm in England. He spent most of his life working in **agriculture**. Howard taught at colleges. He also traveled to foreign countries to share his ideas about farming. Over time, he developed a philosophy about the best way to farm. He said that to create and keep healthy soil, one had to follow "the Law of Return." That means to take the waste products from the land (such as grass clippings, leaves, and food scraps) and put them back into the ground. Howard created his own personal recipe for **compost** and how to use it to help the soil.

The term *organic farming* was created in 1940. It was often used by Jerome Rodale. He read the works of Howard and was inspired to buy a farm near Allentown, Pennsylvania. He experimented with different kinds of compost and grew organic crops. In 1942, Rodale began publishing a magazine called *Organic Farming and Gardening*. It gave farmers suggestions and advice. People began reading his works.

Compost can be made inexpensively from things such as kitchen scraps and fallen leaves.

Farmers were eager for answers, too. For generations, they had been planting crops in the same fields year after year. This took all of the nutrients out of the soil. Without those nutrients, it became harder and harder for plants to grow. Water and sunshine were not enough. In addition, when weeds or pests invaded crops, farmers would fight back. Unfortunately,

Colorado potato beetles are one crop pest that is difficult to get rid of.

the chemicals and **pesticides** that they used harmed the soil. It was clear that there had to be a better, healthier way to grow crops. Rodale's ideas pointed to the answer.

By the 1980s, classes in organic farming were offered at agricultural colleges. Frightening news stories, such as the Alar apple scare, started appearing. This caused interest in organic farming to soar.

LEARNING & INNOVATION SKILLS

Did you know that animals can also be raised organically? On an organic farm, animals are given special feed. It has not had any chemicals, **hormones**, antibiotics or other medications added to it. The animals have a lot of room to move around. They also have frequent access to the outdoors. This provides the animals with a healthy lifestyle. On many large, nonorganic farms, this is not the case. Animals are kept in small, crowded spaces. They may never see the outside. Do you think that the way animals are raised changes the quality of their food products?

As the years went by, more farmers began using organic practices. Organic products began showing up in grocery stores. Interest in buying foods that were grown without dangerous chemicals grew quickly.

In 1990, the Federal Organic Foods Production Act was passed. It established national standards for organic products. This reassured people that each organic product met a certain set of requirements.

21ST CENTURY CONTENT

People disagree about whether or not organic foods are healthier than other foods. Foods grown organically are better for the environment. But are they better for you? Many people say they probably are. But some people argue that any traces of pesticides on nonorganic produce are too small to cause health problems. Others say that there isn't enough evidence to prove that organic food is more nutritious. People also disagree about which option tastes better. It seems that this debate will continue for now. What do you think? Are organic foods healthier than foods grown in other ways?

Ladybugs eat harmful insects, such as aphids. They can help protect crops without hurting the plants.

Organic farming relies on healthy **biodiversity**. Birds, beneficial insects, and other animals are used for pest control. This, in turn, benefits the surrounding environment. In the 21st century, organic farming is here to stay.

CHAPTER TWO
EARLY MORNING CHORES

The morning starts early at Brent and Regina Beidler's organic farm in Vermont. The farm has 100 open acres (40.5 hectares) used for pasture, hay, and other crops. It also

Grain used to be harvested by hand. Combines make the job easier and faster.

has 45 acres (18 ha) of woods. The Beidlers' focus is on dairy farming. They also grow wheat, dried beans, sweet corn, potatoes, and tomatoes.

Brent wakes up at 4 A.M. He heads out to the barn to bring in 35 cows for milking. It takes about an hour and a half to milk the cows. He finishes that, and by the time he washes the equipment and feeds the calves, it is 6:30 A.M. He and Regina put their daughter on the school bus. They are back in the barn before 7:00 A.M.

Together they move the portable fence and let the cows out for a breakfast of chemical-free green grass. For the next hour, Brent and Regina clean the barn. This includes sweeping and putting down fresh bedding and feed. As the seasons change, so does the work. In the fall, Brent and Regina's hours are spent harvesting wheat. Hay is taken to a neighbor's barn for stacking. Brent heads out to check on other bales of straw. Are they dry enough to be brought in yet? No, not quite. The black beans are ready though. So after lunch, he heads out to the field with his **combine** to start harvesting them. When he is done, he comes inside to answer e-mails and phone calls. Then he welcomes his daughter home from school.

The sun begins to set. It is time to bring the cows back in for the evening milking. This and other chores keep Brent and Regina busy until dinnertime. Regina says, "After dinner, we usually settle in for a quiet evening and then nod off on the couch before heading to bed and getting ready for the routine to begin again the next morning. It is more than a job—it's our life!"

In another part of the country, Marie Tedei also begins the day early. She is the owner of Eden's Organic Garden Center in Texas. It is a small farm with 1.5 acres (0.6 ha) of broccoli, cauliflower, brussels sprouts, lettuce, cabbage, and

Organic farms are often small, family-owned farms.

kale. By 5 A.M., Marie grabs her flashlight and wheelbarrow. She loads it with plants and organic soil. The weatherman said rain was less than two hours away. So she shot out of bed and moved, as she put it, "much faster than I've ever rushed out of the house for any regular job, that is for sure. Ah, life on the farm." She wants to put the plants in the ground before the rain arrives. She has had seedlings in pots for weeks. Now that the rain is coming, she wants to get them securely in the soil.

LEARNING & INNOVATION SKILLS

The next time you go into your local grocery store, look around the produce section. Is there a section that is labeled "organic"? Compare the price of organic vegetables to the price of the regular vegetables. You will find that the organic vegetables are usually more expensive. Would you be willing to pay more for organic produce? Why or why not?

21ST CENTURY CONTENT

Many organic farmers are part of a system called Community Supported Agriculture (CSA). Customers pay CSA farms a set amount of money. In return, they receive a share of fresh produce every week during a growing season. Farmers and customers both benefit from this system. Farmers have a steady group of customers. Customers receive fruits and vegetables that are grown locally. Why buy food that is grown locally? It takes less fuel to ship food that is grown nearby. In addition, produce that is eaten soon after harvest generally provides more nutrients and better taste. Becoming a CSA farm shareholder is a great way to support farmers in your community.

Marie kneels on the ground and begins planting. The only sound she hears is the roosters letting others know that sunrise is moments away. A flash of lightning lights the sky. Marie keeps planting. Then a second flash is followed by a downpour. She finishes in the rain, grateful for the way it soaks in perfectly. Marie loves her work and says, "When you watch nature, from the seeds up, it gives you a whole new perspective and appreciation for many, many things."

Labels help a farmer identify the seedlings that have been planted.

Lady's Finger

CHAPTER THREE
BECOMING AN ORGANIC FARMER

Schools for organic farming did not exist a few years ago. Now, however, a few colleges offer organic farming degrees.

Farmers take pride in their work.

You do not need a college degree to become an organic farmer. But you do need a wide set of interests and abilities. To become an organic farmer, you should:

- find enjoyment in working outside
- have a basic understanding of soils
- be willing to work in all kinds of weather
- have patience
- be willing to work seven days a week
- be able to work many long hours for days in a row
- be capable of getting up very early in the morning
- have physical strength
- enjoy many different types of animals
- have a true interest in how to grow things

What topics should you know about?

- Animal health
- Equipment use and repair
- Soil chemistry and soil health
- **Irrigation**
- Crop rotation
- Uses of solar power, **turbines**, and other energy alternatives
- How to create and use compost
- How to grow plants without pesticides and other chemicals

Do you want to start learning more about organic farming now? There are a number of things you can do. Find a farm that will let you help out. Call and ask if you and your parents could come out for a visit. Ask what opportunities are available for you to learn. Maybe you can work there as a volunteer.

If you don't live near any farms, there are other things you can do. Start your own small garden, if it is possible.

The best way to learn about organic farming is through hands-on experience.

See how much you can grow organically. Or see if there is a community garden in your area. If so, volunteer to help there. This will help you become familiar with farming tools such as hoes, shovels, and other hand tools.

There may be an agricultural program in your school. It might be (4-H), Future Farmers of America, or another organization. Participating in these programs can teach you important lessons about farming.

 LIFE & CAREER SKILLS

Is there a college in your area that offers agricultural programs or degrees in organic farming? Ask your parents if you can take a tour of the school. You can pick up a lot of information there. Make sure to ask questions as you tour the facility. You can talk to the tour guide, students, or even professors in the field. Asking questions to learn more about subjects that interest you is an important skill. It will be useful no matter what career you choose.

Go to the library and check out books and magazines about organic farming. It is important that you understand the basic principles behind organic farming. Read some of the history and the science behind it.

Becoming an organic farmer is a big responsibility. You need to love nature, and you must have a passion for keeping the planet clean, safe, and healthy.

 LIFE & CAREER SKILLS

Crop rotation is an important aspect of organic farming. Crop rotation means that farmers choose different types of crops to grow on their land each season. They might plant onions one year and carrots and tomatoes the next year. Why? Different crops take different nutrients from the soil. Crop rotation helps restore the soil's nutrients.

Which crops are best to use in a rotation cycle? What are some other benefits of crop rotation? Do some research. Taking steps to learn more about crop rotation shows that you are serious about becoming a successful organic farmer.

Organizations such as 4-H hold competitions for raising vegetables and livestock.

CHAPTER FOUR
FARMING FUTURES

I f you want to be an organic farmer, your timing could not be better. The future of the field is opening up in

Nearly any kind of food can be produced organically, including nuts.

many ways. It is growing stronger every year. More classes are being offered, and more degrees are being created. Washington State University in Pullman has created a major in Organic Agriculture. Michigan State University in East Lansing has created an organic farming certification program. New programs at other universities are sure to follow.

21ST CENTURY CONTENT

Hunger has been a problem in Africa for many years. Little rain, large populations, and poor soil make it difficult to grow enough food. A study by the United Nations points to organic farming as one possible solution. A review of 114 farming projects in 24 African countries showed surprising results. Crop yields more than doubled where organic methods were used. The soil was healthier and was able to hold moisture longer. As Achim Steiner, of the United Nations' Environment Programme, stated, "The potential contribution of organic farming to feeding the world may be far higher than many had supposed."

In the United States, interest in organic products has grown by about 20 percent each year for the past several years. Almost half of Americans say they believe organic products are good for them and for the environment. Experts predict that this trend will keep growing. As the demand for organic products grows, the need for skilled organic farmers will grow, too.

Running an organic farm is hard work, but it can also be very rewarding.

Organic farming can help people around the world, from African farmers to American consumers.

In 2005, people spent more than $12.8 billion buying organic products. More than 2 million acres (809,371 ha) throughout the country are dedicated to organic farming. They are tended by 13,000 organic farmers.

If you pay attention, you will see organic products in many different places. Even large department store chains such as Walmart have made room for them. Grocery stores such as Whole Foods and Trader Joe's focus on organic foods and other healthy products. These chains have grown quickly in recent years.

Being an organic farmer today is exciting. It is an area that is changing constantly. New studies are being done, and better techniques are being developed. Demand for organic products is likely to keep growing. People want food that they know they can trust. They do not want to wonder, as Emily Hall did, if the apples they are putting in their children's lunch boxes are safe or not.

SOME FAMOUS
ORGANIC FARMERS

Rachel Carson (1907–1964) was a nature writer. Her most famous work is *Silent Spring*. Her research and writing helped people understand the threats that pesticides pose to the environment.

Prince Charles Philip Arthur George (1948–) is the Prince of Wales. He is a well-known organic farming advocate. His 1,100 acres (445 ha) in Gloucestershire are all organic, and he has written about the process. He is considered by many to be a modern "hero of the environment."

Sir Albert Howard (1873–1947) was known as the pioneer of the organic movement. He spent his life learning and teaching about natural farming techniques. He was one of the first people to introduce the idea that disease in animals and humans comes from unhealthy soil and the foods grown in it.

Jerome Irving Rodale (1898–1971) was an author and avid fan of organic farming. He experimented with many different techniques and wrote about them in several books. He also published *Organic Farming and Gardening* magazine.

Carl Sprengel (1787–1859) played an important role in developing the Law of the Minimum. This idea focuses on the proper balance of elements that is needed to help plants grow and develop.

GLOSSARY

agriculture (AG-rih-kuhl-churr) the science of cultivating land, growing crops, and raising livestock

biodiversity (bye-oh-duh-VURS-it-ee) a condition in nature in which a large variety of living things lives in a certain area

combine (KOM-bine) a harvesting machine that cuts, threshes, and cleans grain

compost (KOM-pohst) a mixture of decaying organic materials such as leaves, vegetables, and manure that is added to the soil to make it richer

hormones (HOR-mohnz) substances made in the glands in the bodies of humans and other animals that affect growth and development

irrigation (ihr-uh-GAY-shuhn) the supply of water to crops by artificial means such as pipes and sprinklers

pesticides (PESS-tuh-sydz) chemicals used for destroying pests such as insects

turbines (TUR-bynz) machines with a rotor and blades driven by steam, water, hot gas, or air

FOR MORE INFORMATION

BOOKS

Langley, Andrew. *Is Organic Food Better?* Chicago: Heinemann Library, 2009.

Miller, Debra A. *Organic Foods*. Detroit: Thomson Gale, 2008.

WEB SITES

EcoKids: My Visit to an Organic Farm
www.ecokidsonline.com/pub/eco_info/topics/landuse/organic_farm/index.cfm
Take an online tour of an organic farm

Kids Organic Club
www.organics.org/kids_club.php
Find fact sheets about organic farming

Rodale Institute—Proving That Healthy Soil Grows Healthy Plants
www.rodaleinstitute.org/node/464
Try this science experiment that shows how the quality of soil affects the growth of plants

INDEX

ABOUT THE AUTHOR

Tamra B. Orr is a full-time author living in the beautiful Pacific Northwest. She has written more than 150 books for readers of all ages and learns something new every single time. She is the mother of four and earned her degree from Ball State University. In her rare spare time, she likes to read, write old-fashioned letters, and visit the coast with her family.